CW01206790

Marvelous Marty
and his Clever Cat Lou

A Pawsitive story of Autism

By Ellen Safranek

Copyright © 2023 Ellen Safranek

All rights reserved. This book or any portion thereafter may not be reproduced or used in any manner whatsoever without the express written permission of the publishers except for the use of brief quotations in a book review.

ISBN: 979-8-218-2758-6 (Ebook)
ISBN: 979-8-218-26833-6 (Hardback)
ISBN: 979-8-218-27257-9 (Paperback)

Illustrated by Nadezhda at GetYourBookIllustrations
Cover and Book Design by Kezia at GetYourBookIllustrations
www.getyourbookillustrations.com

First Print 2023

Dedicated to my son and best buddy
for life – I love you ♥

To all the wonderful people that
surround us, fill our lives with love,
and make us better people.

And, of course, to our furry loves
who help keep us brave.

Hi Friends,

I wrote this book to explain to my son that he has autism and to help him make sense of his world. I hope that you will use it to do the same with your kiddo.

Lou the cat is based on a real-life fabulous feline who has been a consistent source of comfort for my son. Our kitty has always been key to making new adventures more approachable. Use Lou's prompts to communicate with your child about their world and any new experiences they may be facing.

As you move through the book, work with your child to find your own pictures that reflect how they would feel in similar situations. Paste those pictures right into the book. The result will be a book about your child and their unique experiences and feelings.

For some, starting this kind of conversation with their child seems scary, it was for me. Please know that this is a journey. Helping our children learn and practice strategies that will help them grow, adapt, and be proud of themselves is something we do as part of that journey.

I've been on this journey with my son for a while now. I have learned that, while there are challenges, that's ok... that's ok because we can embrace strategies to help our children manage and overcome challenges, to enjoy our world together. After all, all kiddos have things that they struggle with... autism just happens to be ours.

All the best,

Ellen

Hi! My name is Marty.
I have bright blue eyes.
I am incredibly smart.
I am very funny.
I have Autism. And I'm O.K!
Let me show you my world.

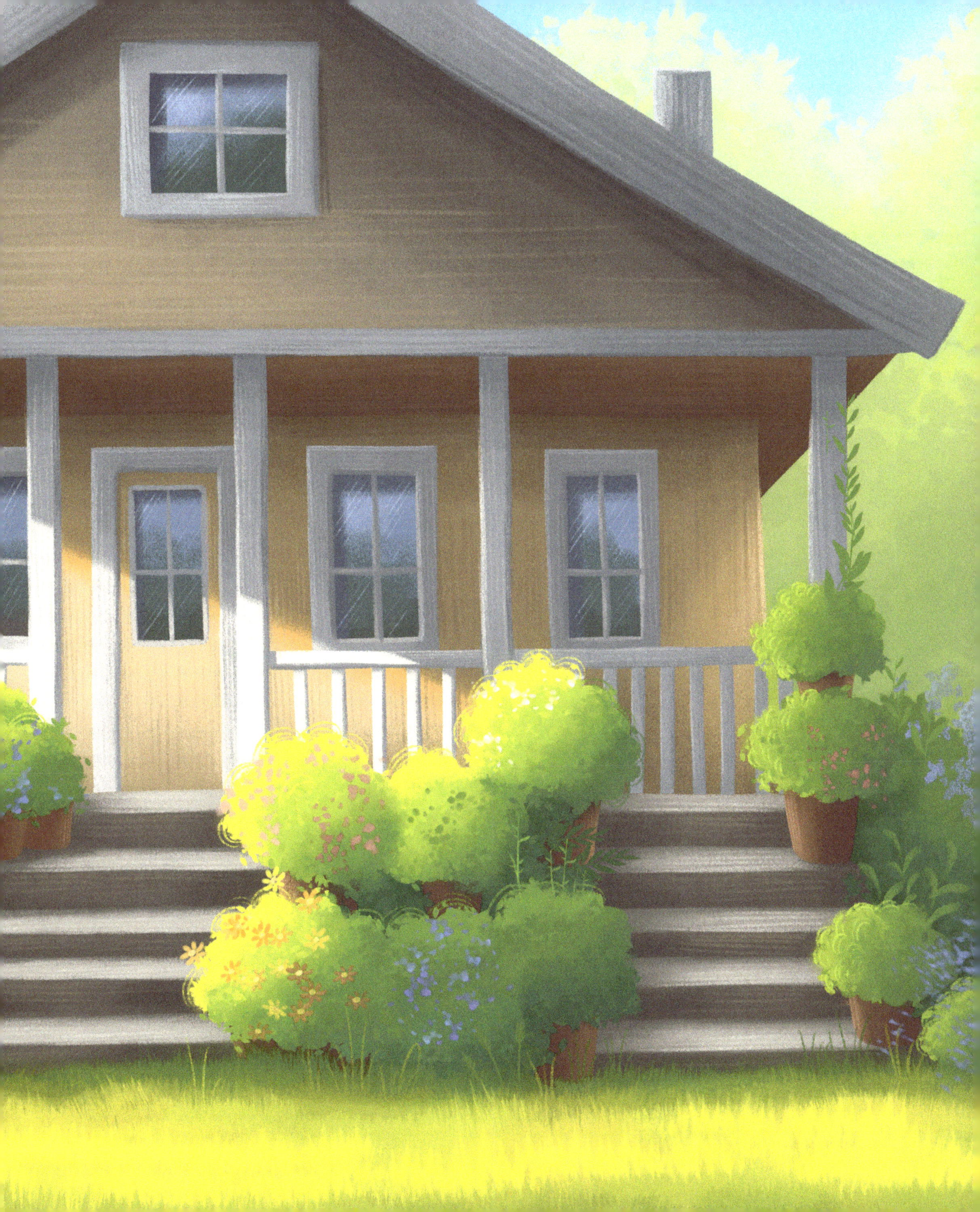

Here is a picture of me with my best friend.

Do you have a picture with your **best friend?**

Hi! I'm Lou and I'm going to help Marty explain Autism.

Autism means my brain works a little differently.

Have you ever felt this way?

People with autism can have problems making sense of the world

Some words can make me feel tense and unhappy.

Autism can mix up your senses a bit.

Can you feel words? Do you smell colors? Is there a sense you have that seems a little different to you?

Other words can tickle and make me laugh.

You're not the only one who experiences the world in an uncommon way.

Woah cool! Can you name something you experience that's unique to you?

A lot of people with autism do!

Autism is not rare. There are plenty of people like us.
But I am *unique*... just like you.
I have my own strengths and weaknesses.

All kids do.

What's your superpower?

me and my dad

My Mom and Dad say that I am an incredible son...

Do you have pictures with people you **love?**

me and my mom

My teacher says that I am a wonderful student...

Do you have a furry friend?

And my pets say that I am especially kind, thoughtful, and loving.

I love my cat!

But... I am also a *bit sensitive* to the world around me. For example, lots of noise and flashing lights can make me feel nervous or scared.

But that's ok...

...that's ok because I'm *learning* to use tools like covering my ears when there are loud noises.

Having tools helps me make my world a better place for me.

You're ok... you're learning.

Sometimes I feel uncomfortable in crowded places, and I want to hide.

But that's ok...

...that's ok because I've learned that I can find a nice quiet place and **take a break**.

Where's your favorite quiet place?

I know I don't always look people
in the eye when they talk to me.

But that's ok...

How do you let people know you're paying attention?

Hey, he sees me!

...that's ok because I'm learning that when I look at people when they talk, they know that I'm paying attention.

You know what else? New clothes can make me feel nervous around friends, and those silly tags in my shirts can hurt.

But that's ok...

Here to **help**, bestie!

...that's ok because now I practice wearing new clothes before I go to school, and those silly tags can be removed!

Sometimes I like to say things over and over again or watch movies in my mind – especially when I'm **uncomfortable** or don't know what's happening next. I know that sometimes this can be inappropriate.

But that's ok...

What kinds of things do you think about?

...that's ok because I'm learning that sometimes I have to **pause** the thoughts and pictures in my mind and save them for later. Also... I can **use a schedule** to help me know what's happening next.

I know that sometimes I hog the conversation or interrupt while someone is talking.

But that's ok...

...that's ok because I'm learning how to take turns when talking with others. I'm also learning that if I interrupt while someone is talking, I need to say "excuse me" and wait my turn.

I know that when I get excited, my body wants to **jump and bounce**. And, when I get frustrated, I need to **grind my teeth or bang my head**.

But that's... o... k...

In 1... 2... 3... and out 1... 2... 3...

...that's ok because I've learned that deep breaths help me calm my body, so I don't feel so frustrated. Breathing helps me feel more in control.

I know sometimes I may talk or stand too closely to people, and this can make **them** feel *uncomfortable*.

But that's ok...

...that's ok because I've learned that people like to keep a **bubble of personal space** around them that makes them feel safe.

"This bubble thing is *tricky*. How much space do you need? Does your bubble change?"

Everyone's bubble may be a little different in size and it can change based on the activity or the people.

I have lots of things to learn... everyone does!
And that's ok...

...that's ok because I have a lot of people who **love** me and want to help me learn. With their love and support, I can be brave and try new things. That's how **we** grow.

I have autism...

...and that's ok